The
MELBOURNE

D0784682

Pocket Guidebook

DISCLAIMER

Whilst all care has been taken by the publisher and author to ensure that the information is accurate and up to date, the publisher does not take responsibility for the information published herein. The recommendations are those of the author, and as things get better or worse, places close and others open, some elements in the book may be inaccurate when you get there. Please write and tell us about it so we can update in subsequent editions.

Cover Picture : Melbourne Tram in St. Kilda Road, Melbourne City.
Inside Cover: Melburnians' favourite game, Australian Football.

MAPS

Melbourne City area - pages 4-5.

Melbourne City -
Accommodation   page 20.

Melbourne City -
Restaurants   page 28.

CONTENTS

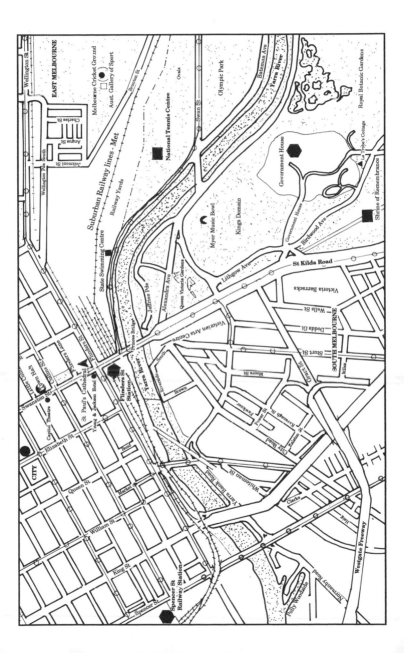

INTRODUCTION

BRIEF

Melbourne, the capital of Victoria, is situated on the shores of Port Phillip Bay.

Victoria is called the Garden State, and its capital city certainly does its share to live up to that reputation. It has tree-lined boulevards and acres of parkland on the banks of the Yarra River, which flows through the city.

Melbourne is Australia's second largest city, and is considered by some to be the nation's sporting, dining, fashion and cultural capital. It also has a reputation for exciting nightlife.

CLIMATE

Melbourne's climate is midway between maritime and continental, and is very changeable.
Average temperatures: January max 26C (79F) - min 14C (57F); July max 13C (55F) - min 6C (43F).
Average annual rainfall: 656mm.
The driest months are June to August.

PEOPLE

Melbourne has a population of 3,080,800, and more than 25% of these people were born overseas. Consequently, the city has a cosmopolitan society, which is reflected in the wide range of restaurants available.

HISTORY

In the early 1800s, officials in Britain and New South Wales were worried about French exploration of the south coast of Australia. To prevent any attempt these explorers might make to begin a settlement, a small expedition of convicts, soldiers and settlers under the command of Colonel Collins was sent to occupy Port Phillip in 1803. After only a few months, Collins decided to move his people to the Van Diemen's Land (Tasmania), where he chose and named Hobart Town as the site for a settlement.

The same fears arose in 1826, and a garrison manned by convict labour was established at Western Port on Corio Bay in Port Phillip. It too was short-lived.

In 1835, while settlers and business men in Launceston and Hobart were thinking about forming a settlement at Port Phillip, John Batman formed the Port Phillip Association, and purchased 100,000 acres in the area from the aborigines for twelve tomahawks and other trade goods. (On the north side of Flinders Street, between Market and William Streets, there is a small plaque in the pavement marking the place where Batman stood when he declared that it was a good place for a village).

In the same year, John Pascoe Fawkner, the son of a convict, acquired land at the northern head of Port Phillip, and there began a brawl between the two men as to who was the real pioneer of the district.

1830s & 40s

In 1836, Governor Bourke vetoed Batman's purchase, and appointed Captain William Lonsdale as resident magistrate of the rapidly-growing settlement. In 1839 the surveyor Robert Hoddle drew up a plan for a city of rectangles within a square mile, with the main thoroughfare running due north, thus exposing future residents to the hot north winds in summer and the cold south winds in winter. The town was named Melbourne after the British Prime Minister.

By 1840 there were 10,291 people living in the district.

The Australian Colonies Government Act was passed in August 1850, and it constituted the Port Phillip district as a separate colony, with La Trobe as its first Lieutenant-Governor. When the news reached Melbourne, in November, there were wild celebrations which lasted a full week. Also, during that week the Prince's Bridge over the Yarra was officially opened to traffic.

Discovery of Gold

In August, 1851, T. Hiscock discovered gold at Ballarat, and people arrived from all over the world seeking their fortune. The consequent Eureka Uprising gave the new government its first major challenge.

By 1880, Melbourne had a population of 250,000 people, and 'more than 1000 gaslights'. The following ten years saw an unparalleled building boom and a period known as 'Marvellous Melbourne'. The magnificent domed Exhibition Hall was built for the International Exhibition of 1880.

Today

The first skyscraper built in Melbourne was ICI House at 1 Nicholson Street. The city skyline now is a mixture of modern towers and old government buildings. The Yarra River has had its course straightened, bridges have been built across it, the docks have been moved closer to Port Phillip Bay, and the western swamps that presented such a problem to the early planners, have been drained. There is not much comparison now with the early settlement of Port Phillip.

FESTIVALS

While some of the following are not festivals as such, they are important annual events that draw crowds of people and attract a lot of interest, not only in Melbourne but throughout the country.

January

Melbourne Folkfest.

The Folkfest is an extravaganza of multi-cultural activities held over nine nights at twenty-two 'pavilions' located throughout Melbourne's suburbs. Each venue presents a friendly environment of spirited song and dance, mouth-watering cuisines and colourful displays. Most provide four shows nightly, lasting about 90 minutes, so more than one pavilion can be visited in one night. Commencing in 1993, this is Australia's newest festival.

The Australian Open.

Held over fourteen days and nine nights, the Australian Tennis Championship is the only Grand Slam title held in Australia. The venue is Flinders Park National Tennis Centre, Batman Avenue, and for more information, phone 655 1175.

February

The Melbourne Music Festival.

A ten day celebration of contemporary music with the emphasis on Australian talent. There are performances, workshops, seminars and conferences held at various indoor and outdoor venues throughout Melbourne. More information can be obtained from The Manager, Vic Rock Foundation, ph 696 2022.

March

The Moomba Festival.

Moomba means 'getting together and having fun' and Melbourne swings with many events from sports to arts held all over the city. The festival has been held annually since 1953, and more information can be obtained from the Moomba Festival Operations Manager, ph 376 1244.

April

The Melbourne International Comedy Festival.

This festival offers around three weeks of organised mayhem and hilarity in the heartland of Australian comedy. Held annually at various locations in Melbourne since 1986, it includes music, exhibitions, shows, late night venues, stand-up comics, etc. For more information contact the Festival Manager, ph 417 7711.

June

Melbourne International Film Festival.

A world acclaimed film festival, it has been held annually since 1951 at various cinemas around Melbourne. For more information contact the Director, ph 662 2953.

September

Melbourne International Festival of the Arts.

Formerly known as the Spoletto Festival, it is also held at various venues around the city over a period of two weeks. Further information can be obtained from the General Manager of the Festival, ph 614 4484.

September

The Royal Melbourne Show.

An annual event which draws about 800,000 visitors each year to the Royal Melbourne Showgrounds in Epsom Road, Ascot Vale. Activities include stud livestock judging, wood chopping contests, arts and crafts, rides, free activities and displays, ph 376 3733.

October

The Caulfield Cup.

Australia's hardest handicap horse race is run over 2400m, and was first contested in 1879. Caulfield Racecourse is in Station Street, ph 572 1111.

November

The Melbourne Cup.

On the first Tuesday in November all of Australia grinds to a halt for the running of this prestigious horse race. Those lucky people in Melbourne, who are given the day off work, head for Flemington Race Course; those elsewhere gather together around the closest TV or radio, to urge their horse to the winning post. People who don't know one end of a horse from the other, line up at the local TAB to put a dollar on their favourite; and everyone, from school children to folk in retirement villages, buys a ticket in the local 'sweep' (sweepstake). The first Melbourne Cup was run in 1861.

TRAVEL TIPS

AIRPORT FACILITIES

Tullamarine International Airport is serviced by over 20 international carriers. It is about 20km out of the city, and a Skybus operates between Tullamarine and the terminal at 97 Franklin Street, ph 663 1400. The Frankston and Peninsula Airport Shuttle, ph 786 6888, takes passengers to that area, and there are also shuttle buses for the eastern suburbs, ph 793 4298.

Facilities at the airport include: duty free shops on arrivals and departures levels; foreign currency exchange; post office; coffee shops, lounges, bars; car rental; telephones; and information offices.

AIRLINE OFFICES

Following is a selection of airlines, with flight confirmation phone numbers:
Air New Zealand, ph 654 3311
British Airways, ph 603 1133
Cathay Pacific, ph 607 1111
Qantas, ph 805 0111
Singapore Airlines, ph 605 2555
United Airlines, ph 602 2544

ALCOHOL

The legal age for purchasing alcohol is 18 years. Children are permitted into lounge bars where food is served as long as they are accompanied by an adult. Many hotels have outside 'beer gardens' and children are allowed entry to these.

The legal limit of blood alcohol while driving is 0.05 per cent.

CHURCHES & TEMPLES

Anglican
St Paul's Cathedral, Flinders Street, ph 650 3791.

St Peter's, Albert Street, ph 662 2391.

Baptist
174 Collins Street, Melbourne, ph 650 1180.

Catholic
St Patrick's Cathedral, Albert Street, East Melbourne, ph 662 2233.

St Augustine's, 631 Bourke Street, ph 629 7494.

St Francis', cnr Elizabeth & Lonsdale Streets, ph 663 2495.

Church of Christ
194 Little Lonsdale Street, ph 663 3884.

Jewish
East Melbourne Synagogue, Albert Street, East Melbourne, ph 662 1372.

Melbourne Synagogue, Toorak Road, South Yarra, ph 866 2255.

Lutheran
Lutheran German Church, 22 Parliament Place, ph 654 5743.

Presbyterian
717 Flinders Lane, ph 629 7083.
Russell Street, ph 650 9903.

Salvation Army
Salvation Army Temple, 69 Bourke Street, ph 650 4851.

Scots Church
99 Russell Street, ph 650 9903.

Uniting Church
St Michael's, 120 Collins Street, ph 654 5120.

COMMUNICATIONS

Mail

The General Post Office is at the corner of Elizabeth and Bourke Streets, and is open Mon-Fri 8.15am-5.30pm, Sat 9am-noon. A mail holding service is available, and for details phone 660 1366.

Suburban post offices are open Mon-Fri 9am-5.30pm.

The cost of postage for mailing a postcard by Air Mail is:
to
New Zealand - 70c
Singapore - 80c
Hong Kong and Japan - 90c
United States & Canada - 95c
United Kingdom - $1.00

Telephone

Public telephones are found in hotels, shops and cafes, and on street corners. **A local call costs 30c,** irrespective of the length of the call.

Calls to places out of the Melbourne 03 Area Code are time-charged, and the fee varies with the distance involved, and the time of day the call is placed.

The cheapest time to ring is from 6pm Sat to 8am Mon, or every day from 10pm to 8am, when savings are up to 60% of the day-time rate.

The area codes for places outside the Melbourne area are found in back of the A-K White Pages of the Melbourne Telephone Directory.

Overseas calls can be dialled direct, and the International Access Code is 0011. The International Direct Dial country and area codes are also found in the back of the A-K White Pages of the Melbourne Telephone Directory. *The Country Code for Australia is 61.*

Country Direct is a service which enables travellers in Australia to gain direct access to telephone operators in their home country so as to make telephone credit card or reverse charge (collect) calls. It may be necessary to insert the local call fee to make a Country Direct call. The telephone numbers are found in the Calling Information section in the front of the A-K White Pages of the Melbourne Telephone Book, and include:

Canada - 0014 881 150
Hong Kong - 0014 881 852
Japan - 0014 881 810
New Zealand - 0014 881 640
Singapore - 0014 881 650
UK (BTI) - 0014 881 440
USA(AT & T) - 0014 881 011
USA (MCI) - 0014 881 100
USA (SPRINT) - 0014 881 877

Time Zones

Australian Eastern Standard Time is Greenwich Mean Time + 10 hours. If Daylight Saving is not involved, when it is Noon in Melbourne, the following times are applicable:

Auckland - 2.00pm
London - 2.00am
Los Angeles - 6.00pm (previous day)
New York - 9.00pm (previous day)
Ottawa - 9.00pm (previous day)
Singapore - 10.00am
Hong Kong - 10.00am
Tokyo - 11.00am
Vancouver - 6.00pm (previous day).

Melbourne, and indeed all of Victoria, has **Daylight Saving,** and clocks are put forward one hour at 2.00am on the last Sunday in October every year.

Australian Eastern Summer Time continues until 2.00am on the first Sunday in March, when clocks are put back one hour.

If you decide to ring home to

the Northern Hemisphere when Sydney is not in Daylight Saving, chances are that your country is on Summer Time, so appropriate adjustment must be made to the times mentioned above. It does not make people conducive to accepting the charges for an overseas call if you wake them up at some ungodly hour.

USEFUL TELEPHONE NUMBERS

Emergencies - Fire, Police, Ambulance - 000
Directory Assistance - Local - 013
Country and interstate - 0175

International - 0103
Call enquiries and costs - calls within Australia - 012
International - 0102.
Dental Emergency - 341 0222

MEDIA

Newspapers

Melbourne has three daily newspapers **Mon-Sat**:
The Australian, the national paper - 60c (The Saturday edition is called The Weekend Australian - $1);
The Age - 60c Mon-Fri, 90c Sat;
The Herald-Sun - 60c
On **Sunday**, the choice is between The Sunday Age (90c) and The Sunday Herald Sun (90c).

The Friday edition of The Age has a lift-out section called "Entertainment Guide" which has information on everything that is happening in Melbourne, with programs and venues.

Radio

The commercial AM radio stations are:
3AW - 1278 - News and information
3MP - 1377 - Music and information
3XY - 1422 - Music
3AK - 1500 - Music
3UZ - 927 - Music
3DB - 100 - Music
3EA - 1224 - Multicultural.
The non-commercial station is ABC - 105.7.
The FM radio stations are:
EON - 92.3 - Music
FOX - 101.9 - Music.

Television

GTV9, HSV7, TEN10, ABC2, and SBS 0/28 (multi-cultural).

CONSULATES

Over seventy countries have diplomatic representation in Canberra, the Capital City of Australia, but Consuls can be found in the State capitals. The addresses for those in Melbourne include:

Canada: 1 Collins Street, ph 654 1433.

Great Britain: 90 Collins Street, ph 650 4155.

Japan: 492 St Kilda Road, ph 867 3244.

New Zealand: 60 Albert Road, South Melbourne, ph 696 0399.

United States: 553 St Kilda Road, ph 526 5900.

CREDIT CARDS

All major credit cards are widely accepted. Shops and restaurants have the logos of the cards they accept near the front door, or at the check-out.

Phone numbers to ring in the event of loss or theft of cards are:
American Express - Cards -
008 230 100 (toll free)
Travellers cheques -
008 251 902
(outside business hours -
008 222 000)
Diners Club - 805 4500
Mastercard /Visa/Bankcard-
Advance - 008 023 369
ANZ Bank - 008 033 844
Citibank 008 037 067
Commonwealth Bank -
008 230 111
National Bank - 008 033 103

State Bank (National) -
008 331 011
Westpac Bank - 008 230 141
(A.H. 008 224 402)
Bank of Qld & R & I Bank of WA - contact local office, no Melbourne agent.

Overseas cards -
Overseas Visitors need only contact any of the above.

• *Tip*
If this is all too much, walk into an establishment displaying your credit card symbol and ask the people there to contact 'card authorization' who will connect you to *stolen/lost cards division*.

You should be able to cancel your cards immediately.

ELECTRICITY

Domestic electricity supply throughout Australia is 230-250 volts, AC 50 cycles. Three-pin plugs are fitted to domestic appliances, so 110 appliances, such as hairdryers and lens sterilisers, cannot be used without a transformer. Many of the hotels and motels have adaptor plugs.

ENTRY FORMALITIES

All travellers to Australia need a valid passport, and visitors of all nationalities, except New Zealand, must obtain a visa before arrival. These are available at Australian Embassies, High Commissions and Consular Offices listed in local telephone directories. No vaccinations are required.

Each incoming traveller over the age of 18 is allowed duty free goods to the value of $400, plus one litre of liquor and 200 cigarettes.

EXIT FORMALITIES

There is a departure tax of $20 for everyone over the age of 12 years who is leaving the country by air.

INFORMATION

There is a network of tourist information booths in the city centre with user-friendly computers that are accessible 24 hours a day, seven days a week.

Locations are:
Bourke Street Mall
Outside the Town Hall
Spencer Street Station
Flinders Street Station
Victorian Arts Centre
Cnr Russell & Collins Streets
Cnr Bourke & Elizabeth Streets.
The RACV (Royal Automobile Club of Victoria) has twenty-nine branches throughout the state which offer a comprehensive touring service. Visitors can book their holiday accommodation day tours, rail, coach and air travel, or rent a car, and obtain tourist information and maps.

The branches in the city are at:
422 Little Collins Street,
ph 607 2137;
and 227 Bourke Street,
ph 650 3983.

Members of automobile clubs and associations world-wide can obtain reciprocal car services from the RACV, and the Vehicle Breakdown Service number is 13 1111.

MONEY

Australia uses a decimal currency system with 100 cents equalling one dollar. The notes are in denominations of $100, $50, $20, $10, $5, and coins are $2, $1, 50 cents, 20 cents, 10 cents and 5 cents. The notes come in different sizes and colours, according to denomination, which makes them very easy to distinguish.

• Banks

Banks are open Mon-Thurs 9.30am-4pm, Fri 9.30am-5pm, and most change travellers cheques and foreign currencies.

• *Bureaux de Change*

Thomas Cook:
261 Bourke Street
Mon-Fri: 8.45am-5.15pm
Sat: 9am-4pm
Sun: 9-3pm

257 Collins Street
Mon-Fri 8.45am-5.15pm
Sat: 9am-noon.

PUBLIC HOLIDAYS

These days are designated as Public Holidays in Victoria:
New Year's Day - January 1
Australia Day - closest Monday to January 26
Labour Day - second Monday in March
Good Friday
Easter Saturday
Easter Monday
Anzac Day - April 25
Queen's Birthday - second Monday in June
Christmas Day
Boxing Day.
Melbourne Metropolitan Area has two extra holidays:
Melbourne Show Day - September
Melbourne Cup Day - second Tuesday in November.

TIPPING

• *Tipping is not a way of life Down Under.*

Of course, if you are particularly impressed by the service you have been given, it is OK to tip. If you decide not to, however, you will not be harassed as you would be in some other countries. It is entirely up to you.

Some restaurants add a small percentage to their bills for weekend trading, and some set a minimum account level. The latter is usually to make sure that customers purchase food as well as beverages, and the limit is usually set at the price of the lowest-priced meal.

ACCOMMODATION

For a complete list of accommodation, contact one of the branches of the RACV (see Information section).

As with any big city, accommodation is usually cheaper in the outer suburbs, and that is obviously where you find the caravan parks. Here is a selection of city and inner suburb accommodation, with prices for a double room per night, which should be used as a guide only.

The telephone area code is 03.

5-Star Hotels

Windsor, cnr Spring & Little Collins Street, ph 653 0653 - 171 rooms, restaurant (closed Sun), bistro - $295-350.

Grand Hyatt Melbourne, cnr Collins & Russell Streets, ph 657 1234 - 580 rooms - restaurant, bistro, cocktail lounge, swimming pool, tennis - $330.

Melbourne Hilton on the Park, 192 Wellington Parade, East Melbourne, ph 419 3311 - 405 rooms, restaurant (closed Sun & Mon), bistro, cocktail lounge, swimming pool - $240-395.

The Regent Melbourne, 25 Collins Street, ph 653 0000 - 310 rooms, restaurant, bistro - $280-335.

Sheraton Towers Southgate, 1 Brown Street, South Melbourne, ph 696 3100 - 375 rooms, restaurant (closed Sun & Mon), bistro, cocktail lounge, swimming pool - $295-450.

Southern Cross, cnr Bourke & Exhibition Streets, ph 653 0221 - 298 rooms, restaurant (closed Sun), bistro, cocktail lounge, swimming pool, tennis - $150.

5-Star Serviced Apartments

Station Pier Condominiums, 15 Beach Street, Port Melbourne, ph 647 9666 - 58 one & two bedroom units, swimming pool, tennis - $190-265.

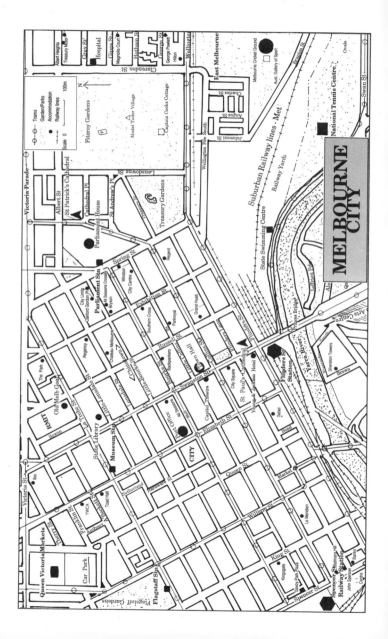

4-Star Hotels

Radisson President, 65 Queens Road, ph 529 4300 - 385 units, restaurant, swimming pool - $175-800.

Le Meridien Melbourne, 495 Collins Street, ph 620 9111 - 232 rooms, restaurant, bistro, swimming pool - $290-310.

Rockmans Regency, cnr Exhibition & Lonsdale Streets, ph 662 3900 - 165 rooms, restaurant (closed Sun), bistro, swimming pool - $295.

Parkroyal on St Kilda Road, 562 St Kilda Road, ph 529 8888 - 220 rooms, restaurant, bistro, cocktail lounge - $215.

The Sebel of Melbourne, 321 Flinders Lane, ph 629 4088 - 59 suites, restaurant - $180-400.

Parkroyal Melbourne on Little Collins Street, 111 Little Collins Street, ph 659 1000 - 283 suites, bistro, cocktail lounge, swimming pool - $175-400.

Bryson, 186 Exhibition Street, ph 662 0511 - 293 rooms, bistro, cocktail lounge, swimming pool - $195-210.

The Park on Exhibition, 333 Exhibition Street, ph 663 3333 - 144 suites, restaurant, swimming pool - $160-187.

Centra Melbourne on the Yarra, cnr Flinders & Spencer Streets, ph 629 5111 - 384 rooms, restaurant, bistro, swimming pool - $150-235.

All Seasons Hotel Swanston, 195 Swanston Street, ph 663 4711 - 143 rooms, restaurant (closed Sun), bistro, cocktail lounge, swimming pool - $125-150.

Eden on the Park, 6 Queens Road, ph 820 2222 - 120 rooms, restaurant - $120-190.

Old Melbourne, 5 Flemington Road, North Melbourne, ph 329 9344 - 216 rooms, restaurant (closed Sun), bistro, cocktail lounge, swimming pool - $113-195.

Savoy Park Plaza, 630 Little Collins Street, ph 622 8888 - 157 rooms, restaurant, cocktail lounge - $98-198.

All Seasons Crossley, 51 Little Bourke Street, ph 639 1639 - 90 units, restaurant - $110-135.

St Kilda Road Travelodge, cnr St Kilda Road & Park Street, ph 699 4833 - 227 units, restaurant, swimming pool - $99-187.

Banks, cnr Spencer Street & Flinders Lane, ph 629 4111 - 190 rooms, restaurant, swimming pool - $99-185.

4-Star Serviced Apartments

Oakford Gordon Place, 24 Little Bourke Street, ph 663 5355 - 59 studio, one & two bedroom & split level units, bistro (closed Sun), pool - $156-345.

Riverside, cnr Flinders Street & Highland Lane, ph 283 7633 - 31 one, two & three bedroom units, light breakfast available - $132 - 190.

Maxims Lygon, 700 Lygon Street, Carlton North, ph 345 3888 - 40 one, two & three bedroom units - $130-190.

3-Star Hotels

The Townhouse, 701 Swanston Street, Carlton, ph 347 7811 - 102 units, restaurant, swimming pool - $129-149.

Batmans Hill, 66 Spencer Street, ph 614 6344 - 86 rooms, restaurant - $115-145.

Chateau Melbourne, 131 Lonsdale Street, ph 663 3161 - 159 rooms, cocktail bar, swimming pool - $110-118.

Ibis, 15 Therry Street, ph 639 2399 - 160 rooms, restaurant - $110.

The John Spencer, 44 Spencer Street, ph 629 6991 - 160 units, restaurant, cocktail lounge - $88-114.

3-Star Motels

The Sheraton Melbourne, 13 Spring Street, ph 650 5000 -

162 units, licensed restaurant, cocktail lounge - $155.

Elizabeth Tower, cnr Elizabeth & Grattan Streets, ph 347 9211 - 114 units, licensed restaurant, swimming pool - $115- 125.

Downtowner, 66 Lygon Street, Carlton, ph 663 5555 - 89 units, unlicensed restaurant - $108-113.

Magnolia Court, 101 Powlett Street, East Melbourne, ph 419 4222 - 21 rooms - $103-110.

Lygon Lodge, 220 Lygon Street, Carlton, ph 663 6633 - 68 units - $90-100.

City Park, 308 Kings Way, South Melbourne, ph 699 9811 - 44 units, licensed restaurant - $89-105.

Marco Polo Inn, cnr Harker Street & Flemington Road, North Melbourne, ph 329 1788 - 67 units, licensed restaurant, swimming pool - $96-98.

Travel Inn, cnr Grattan & Drummond Streets, Carlton, ph 347 7922 - 100 units, licensed restaurant (closed public holidays), swimming pool - $80-140.

Treasury Motor Lodge, 179 Powlett Street, East Melbourne, ph 417 5281 - 21 units - $85-100.

Flagstaff City Motor Inn, 45 Dudley Street, West Melbourne, ph 329 5788 - 39 units - $83-98.

Park Squire Motor Inn, 94 Flemington Road, Parkville, ph 329 6077 - 24 units - $68-88.

Arden, 15 Arden Street, North Melbourne, ph 329 7211 - 61 units - $66-88.

Ramada Inn, 539 Royal Parade (Hume Highway), Parkville, ph 380 8131 - 40 units, unlicensed restaurant - $81.

Astoria City Travel Inn, 288 Spencer Street, ph 670 6801 - 36 units, licensed restaurant, swimming pool - $78.

3-Star Serviced Apartments

Oakford Fairways, 32 Queens Road, ph 867 6511 - 52 one & two bedroom suites, swimming pool, tennis - $145-276

City Gardens, 335 Abbotsford Street, North Melbourne, ph 320 6600 - 126 one, two & three bedroom units, light breakfast ingredients available - $110-200.

Albert Heights, 83 Albert Street, East Melbourne, ph 419 0955 - 35 one bedroom units, swimming pool - $105.

Eastern Town House, 90 Albert Street, ph 418 6666 - 54 one bedroom units - $92.

2-Star Motels

City Limits, 20 Little Bourke Street, ph 662 2544 - 32 units - $85-111.

City Square, 67 Swanston St, ph 654 7011 - 24 units - $90.

Kingsway, cnr Park Street & Eastern Road, South Melbourne, ph 699 2533 - 41 units - $79.

Park Avenue Motor Inn, 461 Royal Parade (Hume Highway), Parkville, ph 380 6761 - 56 units, unlicensed restaurant - $70-80.

George Powlett Lodge, cnr George & Powlett Streets, East Melbourne, ph 419 9488 - 45 units, limited cooking facilities - BLtB $75.

Private Hotels

Kingsgate, 131 King Street, ph 629 3049 - 232 rooms (some with private facilities), licensed restaurant - $50-70.

City Centre, 22 Little Collins Street, ph 654 5401 - 36 rooms with shared facilities, communal cooking facilities - $50.

Miami, 13 Hawke Street, West Melbourne, ph 329 8499 - 100 rooms with shared facilities, communal tea making - $48.

YWCA Family Motel, 489 Elizabeth Street, ph 329 5188 - 56 rooms with private facilities, unlicensed restaurant, swimming pool - $30-58.

Backpackers City Inn, 197 Bourke Street, ph 650 4379 - 29 rooms with shared facilities, licensed restaurant, communal cooking facilities - $32.

Guest Houses

Georgian Court, 21 George Street, East Melbourne, ph 419 6353 - 33 rooms (some with private facilities), unlicensed restaurant (closed Fri-Sat) - $65-85.

Toad Hall, 441 Elizabeth Street, ph 600 9010 - 31 rooms with shared facilities, communal cooking facilities - $40-50.

Youth Hostels

Queensberry Hill YHA, 78 Coward Street, North Melbourne, ph 329 8599 - 91 rooms with shared facilities, bbq , no smoking - $18.

Chapman Street YHA, 76 Chapman Street, North Melbourne, ph 328 3595 - 54 rooms with shared facilities. no smoking - $15.

GETTING AROUND

THE MET

is Melbourne's public transport system, operating trains, trams and buses within the metropolitan area.

The city it divided into three zones and the ticket type depends on which zone you are going to travel in and for how long. Three hour, daily, weekly, monthly or yearly tickets are available at very reasonable prices.

Further information is available from the Met Transport Information Centre, ph 617 0900, or from The Met Shop, 103 Elizabeth Street in the city, or from Chadstone, Chirnside Park, Werribee Plaza and Highpoint City Shopping Centres.

Country travel is controlled by V/Line, who operate rail and coach services from Melbourne to country Victoria daily. For further information phone 619 5000.

Bookings for country and interstate travel may be made in person at major stations, or at the country and interstate terminal, Spencer Street Station, ph 619 5000.

TRANSPORT TO/FROM THE AIRPORT

Skybus Coach Service, ph 335 3066, has a service from the airport to Spencer Street Railway Station, then on to 58 Franklin Street in the city (Sat, Sun and public holidays).

Mon-Fri there is a courtesy bus to Spencer Rail and city hotels, 8.15am-5.15pm.

The return service leaves from 58 Franklin Street Mon-Fri, and from Spencer Railway Station, via 58 Franklin Street Sat-Sun and public holidays, with the hotel courtesy bus running Mon-Fri 9.10am- 4.10pm. The one-way fare is $8.50 adult, $4.50 children 5-14 years.

Tullamarine Bus Lines operate a service for The Met from Moonee Ponds Junction via Essendon Railway Station, Niddrie, Airport West Shopping Town and Tullamarine township to Melbourne Airport and Gladstone Park, ph 617 0900.

Wood's Airport Service, ph (054)47 8210 caters for the Bendigo district.

The Shuttlebus has an express service between Ballarat and the airport, ph (053)35 9770.

The Airport Commuter bus services Heidelberg, Doncaster, Box Hill, Nunawading, Ringwood and Knox City, ph 793 4298.

The Airport bus travels to Dandenong via Glen Iris, Ashburton, Holmesglen, Chadstone, Brandon Park, Rowville and Endeavour Hills, ph 791 2848.

An airport bus stops at Moorabbin, Mentone, Chelsea, Frankston, Mt Eliza, Mornington and Rosebud, ph 786 6888.

The Gull Airport Service travels to Geelong via Werribee and Corio Village, ph (052)22 4966.

TRAMS

Trams are almost synonymous with Melbourne, and are a big draw-card for visitors, but these old-fashioned vehicles still provide transport for thousands of commuters. They are an interesting way to see the city, and are less plagued by breakdown than other forms of transport. It is worthwhile here to give some information on the history of trams, for which we are grateful to National Trust Victoria.

History

Melbourne's first cable tram travelled to Richmond on November 11, 1885, signalling the replacement of the horse-drawn buses then operating extensively within Melbourne. The cable tram network spread to cover 74km, and became the most extensive single integrated system in the world.

The Box Hill and Doncaster Tramway Company introduced Australia's first electric tramway in 1889, and other Melbourne electric tramway systems were developed in the first decades of the twentieth century. In 1919, the Melbourne and Metropolitan Tramways Board was formed to take control of all the city's cable and electric tramways, and to convert them to an all-electric network. In 1923 the MMTB began building a standardized rolling stock - the 'W' Class trams.

Today

Melbourne now has a fleet of 305 'W' Class trams, which have been classified by the National Trust Council - the first time that moveable objects have been classified. Built between 1925 and 1956, these trams have become the pre-eminent symbol of

Melbourne, evident in tourist literature, postcards and souvenir badges.

The trams still serve the original commuter task for which they were built, but there are plans for modernising the fleet and scrapping the vintage trams, except for special tourist routes. This would not be a popular move with the locals, and would rob Melbourne of an identifiable attraction.

TAXIS

Taxis can be hired on the street, at taxi ranks, major hotels, or by phoning one of the taxi companies.

Tariff One, operates between 9am-4pm Mon-Fri, 6am-1pm Sat, and costs 61.7c per km.

Tariff Two operates between 6am-9am and 4pm-midnight Mon-Fri, 1pm-midnight Sat-Sun, plus public holidays, and costs 78.1c per km.

These two tariffs have a Flag Fall of $2.60.

Tariff Three operates midnight-6am daily, and costs 78.1c per km, with a Flag Fall of $3.60.

All tariffs have a service or booking fee of 60c, and waiting time of $18.48 per hour.

Arrow Taxi Service Ltd, ph 417 1111;

Astoria Taxis, ph 347 5511;

Black Cabs and Eastern Group Taxis, ph 567 3333;

D & D Cyma Taxis (Sandown Taxi), ph 791 2111;

Embassy Private Hire Service, ph 320 0320;

Frankston Radio cabs, ph 786 3322;

North Suburban Taxis, ph 480 2222;

Regal Combined Taxis, ph 810 0222;

Silver Top Taxi Service, ph 345 3455;

West Suburban Taxis, ph 689 1144;

River Yarra Water Taxis, ph 018 340 887.

CAR HIRE

There are plenty of car rental agencies, and they accept current international licenses.

ABC Rent a Car, ph 347 9599;

Airport Rent A Car, ph 329 9635;

Avis Rent-A-Car, ph 689 6666;

Budget Rent-A-Car, ph 13 2848;

Budget Chauffeur Drive, ph 429 4900;

Hertz Australia, ph 698 2555;

Luxury Chauffeur Drive, ph 379 7966;

Rent-A-Wreck, ph 329 9295;

Thrifty Rent-A-Car, ph 663 5200.

When driving in Melbourne there are a *few rules about the trams.*

1. Drivers must not obstruct trams, and there are yellow lines on roadways indicating streets in which drivers must keep clear of the tracks when trams are approaching.

2. Drivers must also stop when a tram is picking up or setting down passengers, if there is not a central traffic island.

3. Making a right-hand turn can sometimes be dicey in the city centre. If the intersection has a 'hook turn' sign, the turn has to be made from the left-hand lane when the lights change, to leave the centre of the intersection clear for trams.

BICYCLE HIRE

Melbourne has quite a few bike tracks, and to hire a bike it is best to get in touch with

Bicycle Victoria, ph 670 9911.

EATING OUT

Some people say that Melbourne is the restaurant capital of Australia, and while this is a good way to start an argument with people from other capital cities, there is no doubt that Melbourne does have an excellent range of restaurants. In fact, there are over 3200 of them, representing 70 national cuisines, and if you are intending to stay for a time, it might be a good idea to pick up a copy of *The Age Good Food Guide*, which is available from newsagents.

Restaurants are either **'Licensed'** or **'BYO'**.
Licensed means that the establishment has a licence to sell alcohol;
BYO means 'bring your own' wine, etc, because the restaurant does not have a liquor licence.

Some restaurants, although licensed, allow patrons to supply their own wine (not beer or spirits), which is usually less expensive than paying the mark-up on the wines that the restaurant is legally allowed to add.
Then a *corkage fee* may be added, which will be per bottle or per person, but the end result is usually still less expensive.

Alcohol can be purchased from the *bottle department* of a hotel, or from one of the many *bottle shops* that abound in every suburb.

It is reasonable to say that the price of a bottle of wine in one of these outlets would be less than half the price of the same wine in a restaurant.

Following is a selection of restaurants rated:

Expensive = main course $15+
Moderate = main course $10-$15
Budget = main course under $10.

We have not included the restaurants in the large hotels as everyone knows that they exist, and are much the same the world over with regard to menus and prices.

American

Diner Deluxe, 107 Russell Street, City, ph 650 5438 - BYO -open Mon 7am-3pm, Tues -Thurs 7am-10pm, Fri 7am-midnight, Sat 3pm- midnight, Sun 3-10pm - **Budget** - credit cards accepted.

Harley's Bar & Restaurant, 118 Bourke Street, City, ph 663 2833 - Licensed - open daily 10am-late - **Moderate** - credit cards accepted.

Australian

Colonial Tramcar Restaurant, "Tram Tracks, Melbourne", ph 696 4000 - Licensed - open daily 1-3pm, 5.45-7.15pm, 8.30-11.30pm - the world's first travelling tramcar restaurant, fixed prices which include drinks - **Expensive** - non-smoking - credit cards accepted.

Great Australian Bite, 18 Molesworth Street, North Melbourne, ph 329 3968 - Licensed - open for lunch Mon-Fri, dinner Tues-Sat - **Moderate** - credit cards accepted.

The Last Aussie Fishcaf, 256 Park Street, South Melbourne, ph 699 1900 - Licensed - open Mon-Fri noon-2.30pm, nightly 6-10.30pm - **Moderate** - credit cards accepted.

Metro Brasserie, 41 Bourke St, City, ph 650 2094 - Licensed - open Mon-Fri from noon, Mon-Sat fr. 6pm- **Moderate** - credit cards accepted.

Pancake Parlour, 25 Market Lane, City - BYO - open 24 hours, seven days - **Budget** - credit cards accepted.

The Paragon Cafe, 651 Rathdowne Street, North Carlton, ph 347 7715 - Licensed/BYO - open Mon-Sat 9am-11pm, Sun 9am-10.30pm - **Moderate** - credit cards accepted.

The Prince and The Frog, 161 Spring Street, City, ph 662 1602 - Licensed - open Mon-Sat 4-11pm (from 11am Wed) - **Moderate** - credit cards accepted.

Selby's Restaurant, 356 Victoria Parade, East Melbourne, ph 417 7373 - Licensed/BYO - open for lunch Tues-Fri, dinner Tues-Sat - **Expensive** - credit cards accepted.

The Sheep's Back Diner Deli & Bar, cnr King & Little Collins Streets, City, ph 629 4400 - Licensed - open Mon-Wed 7am-8pm, Thurs 7am-10pm, Fri 7am-1am, Sat 8pm-1am - **Budget** - credit cards accepted.

Tansy's Restaurant, 555 Nicholson Street, Carlton North, ph 380 5555 - BYO - open Tues-Sat from 7.30pm - **Expensive** - credit cards accepted.

Chinese

Bamboo House Restaurant, 47 Little Bourke Street, City, ph 662 1565 - Licensed - open Mon-Fri noon-3pm, Mon-Sat 5.30-11pm, Sun 6-10pm - **Moderate** - credit cards accepted.

Chef Canton, 37-41 Little Bourke Street, City, ph 663 2028 - Licensed/BYO - open Mon-Sat noon-3pm, 6-11pm, Sun 11am-3pm - **Moderate** - credit cards accepted.

Chinese Noodle Shop, 331 Clarendon Street, South Melbourne, ph 699 4150 - BYO - open Mon-Sat 11.45am-3pm, 5-10.30pm, Sun 5.30-9.30pm - **Moderate** - credit cards accepted.

Da Hu Peking Duck Restaurant, 171 Little Bourke Street, City, ph 663 3868 - BYO - open Wed-Mon 11am-3pm, nightly 5.30-11pm - **Budget** - credit cards accepted.

Diamond Crown Chinese Restaurant, 213 Russell Street, City, ph 663 1298 - BYO - open daily 11am-midnight - **Budget** - no credit cards.

Diamond Dynasty, 188 Little Bourke Street, City, ph 663 3001 - BYO - open daily 11am-3pm, 6-11.15pm - **Budget** - credit cards accepted.

Empress of China Restaurant, 120 Little Bourke Street, City, ph 663 1883 - Licensed/BYO - open Mon-Wed noon-3pm, 6-11pm, Thurs-Fri noon-3pm, 6-11.30pm, Sat 6-11.30pm, Sun noon-3pm, 6-10.30pm - **Moderate** - credit cards accepted.

Flower Drum Restaurant, 17 Market Lane, City, ph 662 3655 - Licensed - open Mon-Fri noon-3pm, Mon-Sat 6-11pm, Sun 6-10.30pm - **Expensive** - credit cards accepted.

Fortuna Village Licensed Chinese Restaurant, 235 Little Bourke Street, ph 663 3044 - Licensed - open daily noon-3pm, 6-11.30pm - **Expensive** - credit cards accepted.

Supper Inn Chinese Restaurant, 15-17 Celestial Avenue (off Little Bourke Street), ph 663 4759 - BYO - open daily 5.30pm-2.30am - **Budget** - credit cards accepted.

French

The Balzac, 62 Wellington Parade, East Melbourne, ph 419 6599 - Licensed - open Mon-Fri noon-3pm, Mon-Sat from 6pm - **Expensive** - credit cards accepted.

Bellecour, 502 Queensberry Street, North Melbourne, ph 328 3350 - Licensed/BYO - open Tues-Fri from noon, Tues-Sat from 7pm - **Expensive** - credit cards accepted.

Fanny's Restaurant, 243 Lonsdale Street, ph 663 3017 - Licensed - main dining room open daily noon-3pm, 7pm-midnight; bistro on ground floor open noon-3pm, 6pm-midnight - upstairs, **Expensive** - bistro, **Budget** - credit cards accepted.

Jean Jacques by the Sea, 40 Jacka Boulevard, St Kilda, ph 534 8221 - Licensed - open daily noon-3pm, and from 6pm - **Moderate** - credit cards accepted.

La Chaumiere, 36 Abbotsford Street, West Melbourne, ph 328 1650 - BYO - open Mon-Fri noon-2pm, Mon-Sat from 7pm - **Expensive** - credit cards accepted.

Lynch's, 133 Domain Road, South Yarra, ph 866 5627 - Licensed - open Mon-Fri from noon, Mon-Sat from 6.30pm - **Expensive** - credit cards accepted.

Marchetti's Latin, 55 Lonsdale Street, City, ph 662 1985 - Licensed - open daily noon-3pm and from 6pm - **Expensive** - credit cards accepted.

Marchetti's Tuscan Grill, 401 Little Bourke Street, City, ph 670 6612 - Licensed - open Mon-Fri from noon for lunch and from 5.30pm for dinner, Sat from 6pm - **Moderate** - credit cards accepted.

Maria and Walter's, 166 Rathdowne Street, Carlton, ph 347 3328 - Licensed/BYO - open Tues-Sat from 7pm - **Expensive** - credit cards accepted.

Mietta's, 7 Alfred Place, ph 654 2366 - Licensed - two venues: *restaurant* open for lunch Mon-Fri, dinner Mon-Sat; *lounge* open daily 11am-3am, with food available until 1am - **Expensive** (restaurant), **Budget** (lounge) - credit cards accepted.

Quarter Sessions, 446 Collins Street, ph 670 6588 - Licensed - open Mon-Fri noon-3pm, Mon-Sat from 7pm - **Expensive** - credit cards accepted.

Tolarno Bar & Bistro, 42 Fitzroy Street, St Kilda, ph 525 5477 - Licensed - open Fri-Sat from noon, daily from 6pm - **Moderate** - credit cards accepted.

Greek

Ambrosia, 363 Brunswick Street, Fitzroy, ph 417 7415 - Licensed/BYO - open daily from 6pm - **Moderate** - credit cards accepted.

Fetta's, 11 Johnston Street, Collingwood, ph 417 3960 - BYO - open Sun from noon, daily from 6pm - **Moderate** - credit cards accepted.

Greek Deli & Tavern, 583 Chapel Street, South Yarra, ph 827 3734 - Licensed/BYO - open daily 6pm-1am - **Moderate** - credit cards accepted.

Jim's Greek Tavern, 32 Johnston Street, Collingwood, ph 419 3827 - BYO - open daily 6pm-midnight - **Moderate** - credit cards accepted.

Kaliva, 256 Swan Street, Richmond, ph 428 7028 - BYO - open daily noon-3pm, 5pm-midnight - **Budget** - credit cards accepted.

Nicosia Kebab House, 250 Glenferrie Road, Malvern, ph 509 9823 - BYO - open daily 5pm-midnight - **Budget** - credit cards accepted.

Stalactites Restaurant, 177-183 Lonsdale Street (cnr Russell Street), ph 663 3316 - Licensed/BYO - open 7 days 24 hours - **Budget** - credit cards accepted.

Tsindos The Greek's Restaurant, 197 Lonsdale Street, ph 663 3194 - Licensed/BYO - open Mon-Fri for lunch, nightly for dinner - **Moderate** - credit cards accepted.

Indian

Amber, 73 Acland Street, St Kilda, ph 534 3707 - BYO - open daily 6-11.30pm - **Budget** - credit cards accepted.

Amritas, 174 Rathdowne Street, Carlton, ph 347 7358 - BYO - open Tues-Sun 6.30-11pm - **Budget** - credit cards accepted.

Bedi's Indian Restaurant, 118 Park Street South, ph 690 8233 - Licensed/BYO - open Mon-Fri noon-2.30pm, Mon-Sat 6.30-10pm - **Moderate** - credit cards accepted.

Carlton Curry House, 204 Rathdowne Street, Carlton, ph 347 9632 - BYO - open Tues-Sat 5.30-11pm - **Budget** - credit cards accepted.

India House Restaurant, 401 Swanston Street, ph 663 5858 - Licensed/BYO - open Mon-Fri noon-2.30pm, Mon-Sat 6.30-10.30pm - **Moderate** - credit cards accepted.

Rajah of India, cnr King & Rosslyn Streets, West Melbourne, ph 329 8402 - BYO - open Mon-Fri noon-2.30pm, Mon-Sat 6-10.30pm - **Budget** - credit cards accepted.

Shahnai, 359 Brunswick Street, Fitzroy, ph 417 5709 - BYO - open Tues-Sat 6-11pm - **Budget** - credit cards accepted.

International

Hardware Street Cafe, 33 Hardware Street, ph 670 1104 - BYO - open Mon-Fri 8am-6pm - **Budget** - credit cards accepted.

Selby's, 356 Victoria Parade, East Melbourne, ph 417 7373 - Licensed/BYO - open Tues-Fri from noon, Tues-Sat from 6.30pm - **Expensive** - credit cards accepted.

Slattery's, 219 King Street, ph 670 1360 - Licensed/BYO - open Mon-Fri from noon, Mon-Sat from 6pm - **Moderate** - credit cards accepted.

The Treble Clef, 100 St Kilda Road, (Melbourne Concert Hall), ph 617 8264 - Licensed - open Mon-Fri 7am-8pm, Sat 7.30am-8pm, Sun 8am-5pm - **Budget** - credit cards accepted.

Walnut Tree Restaurant, 458 William Street, ph 328 4409 - Licensed - open Tues-Fri noon-3pm, Tues-Sat 7pm-midnight - **Expensive** - credit cards accepted.

Italian

Arrivederci, 191 Nicholson Street, Carlton, ph 347 8252 - Licensed - open Mon-Fri from noon, Mon-Sat from 7pm - **Moderate** - credit cards accepted.

Bortolotto's, 16 Fitzroy Street, St Kilda, ph 525 4066 - Licensed - open daily noon-3pm,6-11pm -**Moderate** - credit cards accepted.

Cafe Di Stasio, 31 Fitzroy Street, St Kilda, ph 525 3999 - Licensed - open daily noon-3pm, 6-11pm - **Expensive** - credit cards accepted.

Cafe Emilia, 1st Floor, 163 Russell Street, ph 663 3672 - Licensed/BYO - open daily noon-3pm, 5.30-11pm - **Budget** - credit cards accepted.

Cafe L'Euro, 499 St Kilda Road, ph 820 3144 - Licensed - open Mon-Fri for lunch, Wed-Fri for dinner - **Moderate** - credit cards accepted.

Caffe e Cucina, 581 Chapel Street, South Yarra, ph 827 4139 - Licensed - open Mon-Fri 7.30am-midnight, Sat 7.30am-5pm, 6pm-mid-night, Sun 8.30am-midnight - **Moderate** - credit cards accepted.

Caffe Grossi, 199 Toorak Road, Toorak, ph 827 6076 - Licensed - open Mon-Sat noon-3pm and from 6pm - **Expensive** - credit cards accepted.

Centro Cafe, 225 Clarendon Street, South Melbourne, ph 699 5904 - Licensed/BYO - open Mon-Fri from noon, Mon-Sat from 6pm - **Moderate** - credit cards accepted.

Ciao Pizza Napoli, 43 Hardware Street, ph 670 1110 - Licensed/BYO - open Mon-Fri noon-3pm, Mon-Fri 6-10pm - **Moderate** - credit cards accepted.

Copperwood Restaurant, 318 Lygon Street, Carlton, ph 347 1799 - Licensed/BYO - open daily noon-3pm, 5.30 -11.30pm - **Budget** (Bistro), **Moderate** (Restaurant) - credit cards accepted.

Don Giovanni, 358 Brunswick Street, Fitzroy, ph 419 7850 - Licensed - open Mon-Fri from 6.30pm, Sat-Sun from 11am - **Moderate** - credit cards accepted.

Donnini's, 312 Drummond Street, Carlton, ph 347 3128 - BYO - open daily noon -2.30pm, 6-11.30pm- **Moderate** - credit cards accepted.

The Florentino, 80 Bourke Street, City, ph 662 1811 - Licensed - open Mon-Fri noon-2.30pm, Mon-Sat from 6pm - **Expensive** - credit cards accepted.

Il Duca, 10 Wellington Parade, East Melbourne, ph 417 4243 - Licensed/BYO - open Mon-Fri noon-2.30pm, Mon -Sat 6-10pm - **Moderate** - credit cards accepted.

La Contadina, 168-170 Rathdowne Street, Carlton, ph 347 6173 - Licensed/BYO - open Mon-Fri noon-2.30pm, Mon-Sat 6-10.30pm - **Moderate** - credit cards accepted.

Locanda Veneta, 273-279 Cecil Street, South Melbourne, ph 690 5628 - Licensed - open Mon-Fri noon-3pm, Mon-Sat 6-10pm - **Moderate** - credit cards accepted.

Lucattini's, 22 Punch Lane, City, ph 662 2883 - Licensed - open Mon-Fri noon-2.30pm, Mon-Sat from 6pm - **Moderate** - credit cards accepted.

Marchetti's Latin Restaurant, 55 Lonsdale Street, City, ph 662 1985 - Licensed - open daily from noon for lunch, and from 6pm for dinner - **Expensive** - credit cards accepted.

Papa Gino's, 221 Lygon Street, Carlton, ph 347 5758 - BYO - open daily noon-2.30pm, 5pm-midnight - **Budget** - credit cards accepted.

Pasta Veloce, 181-183 Lygon Street, Carlton, ph 347 4273 - Licensed/BYO - open daily noon-midnight - **Budget** - credit cards accepted.

Japanese

Kanpai, 569 Chapel Street, South Yarra, ph 827 4379 - Licensed/BYO - open daily noon-midnight - **Budget** - credit cards accepted.

Kenzan Japanese Restaurant, Collins Place, 45 Collins St, City, ph 654 8933 - Licensed - open Mon-Fri from noon, Mon-Sat from 6pm - **Moderate** - credit cards accepted.

Kobe, 170-181 Clarendon Street, South Melbourne, ph 690 2692 - Licensed/BYO - open Mon-Fri noon-3pm, daily 6-11pm - **Budget** - credit cards accepted.

Murasaki Japanese Restaurant, 24 Russell Street, City, ph 654 5437 - Licensed/BYO - open Mon-Fri noon-2.30pm, Mon-Sat 6-10pm - **Moderate** - credit cards accepted.

Stone Garden (Sekitei) Japanese Restaurant, 2nd Floor, 169 Bourke Street, City, ph 654 7373 - BYO - open Tues-Fri noon-2.30pm, Tues-Sun 6-11pm - **Moderate** - credit cards accepted.

Suntory Restaurant, 74 Queens Lane, City, ph 525 1231 - Licensed - open Mon-Fri noon-2pm, Sun noon-2.30pm, Mon-Sat 6-10pm, Sun 6-9.30pm - **Expensive** - credit cards accepted.

Malaysian

Golden Orchids, 126 Little Bourke Street, City, ph 663 1101 - BYO - open Sun-Fri noon-2.30pm, nightly 5.30-10.15pm - **Moderate** - credit cards accepted.

Lat's Malaysian Restaurant, 11 Heffernan Lane (off Little Bourke Street), City, ph 663 2848 - BYO - open daily noon-11pm - **Budget** - credit cards accepted.

Little Malaysia Restaurant, 26 Liverpool Street, City, ph 662 1678 - BYO - open daily 11am-3pm, 5-11pm - **Budget** - credit cards accepted.

Lotus Garden, 208 Little Bourke Street, City, ph 663 7011 - BYO - open daily noon-3pm, 5.30-11pm - **Moderate** - credit cards accepted.

Rasa Sayang, 26 Market Lane, City, ph 663 4667 - BYO - open Mon-Sat noon-3pm, Sun 11am-3pm, Mon-Thurs 5.30-10.30pm, Fri-Sat 5.30-11.30pm, Sun 5.30-10pm - **Moderate** - credit cards accepted.

Specialist

Cafe Swe-Dish, 510 Elizabeth Street, City, ph 663 1910 - Licensed - open daily 8am-4pm, Thurs-Sat 6-10pm - Swedish cuisine - **Moderate** - credit cards accepted.

Champagne Charlie's, 422 Toorak Road, Toorak, ph 827 5936 - Licensed - open Tues-Sun from 6.30pm - modern brasserie cuisine - **Moderate** - credit cards accepted.

Dirty Dick's, 23 Queens Road, City, ph 867 4788 - Licensed - music comedy and 4 course English banquet Mon-Sat 7pm-1am - **Expensive** - credit cards accepted.

Hofbrauhas, 18 Market Lane, City, ph 663 1229 - Licensed - German food and live entertainment - open Tues-Fri noon-2.30pm, Tues-Sat 6-10.30pm - **Expensive** - credit cards accepted.

Kaye's on King Brasserie, 225 King Street, City, ph 642 0102 - Licensed - award-winning cuisine - open Mon-Fri from 8am for breakfast, Mon-Fri from noon for lunch, Tues-Fri from 6pm for dinner - **Moderate** - credit cards accepted.

Fast Food

Anyone who can feel a *Mac Attack* coming on will not be disappointed because there are **seven McDonald's in the city centre,** many in the suburbs, and indeed they are sprinkled all over Victoria.

Kentucky Fried Chicken doesn't have a city location, but is well represented in the suburbs, and **Pizza Hut has two restaurants in Bourke Street,** as well as suburban branches.

NIGHT-LIFE

Melbourne's night-life conjures up images of excitement, colour, action and entertainment. There is a comprehensive range of nocturnal activities to select from, including discos, wine bars, concerts, theatres, cinemas, live bands, night-clubs and much more.

For complete information on who or what is playing where and when, get a copy of the **"Entertainment Guide" in Friday's edition of The Age,** or phone the Entertainment Hotline, 11 566.

Here is a selection of entertainment venues.

Night-Clubs

The Colosseum (formerly Inflation), 60 King Street, City ph 614 6122 - 3 levels catering for all age groups - a Melbourne institution that has undergone extensive refurbishment - open Fri-Sat 9pm-7am - also has under-18, well-supervised, no alcohol disco Sat 1-6pm.

The Grainstore Tavern, 46 King Street, City, ph 614 3570 - live acts upstairs, a video dance club downstairs.

Ivey Restaurant Niteclub, 146-147 Flinders Lane, City, ph 650 1855 - lunch Thurs-Fri, Dinner Wed-Sat, full entertainment Tues-Sun - East/West cuisine - 5-star entertainment complex.

The Metro, 20-30 Bourke Street, City, ph 663 4288 - open Wed-Sat 9pm-5am - eight bars and three dance floors on three levels - live bands.

Monsoons Nightclub, Grand Hyatt, 123 Collins Street, City, ph 657 1234.

Billboard Nite Club, 170 Russell Street, City, ph 663 4991 - open Thurs-Mon 9.30pm-7am - fully licensed restaurant, cocktail bar - best of live and recorded music.

Bars and Pubs

Level One Tapas Bar, 123 Collins Street, City, ph 675 1234 - open Tues-Thurs 5pm-midnight, Fri-Sat 5pm-2am - flamenco guitarist.

Young & Jacksons, 1 Swanston Street, City, ph 650 3884 - open Mon-Thurs 10am-10pm, Fri-Sat 10am-11.30pm - meals Mon-Sat 11am-3pm, 6-9.30pm - home of the once-controversial *Chloe*.

Black Match, 545 Church Street, Richmond, ph 428 5127 - open Mon-Sat noon-1am - meals noon-2.30pm and from 6.30pm - super trendy.

Black Prince, 455 Chapel Street, South Yarra, ph 824 1000 - open Mon-Sat 10am-1am, Sun 10am-11.30 pm - meals noon-2.30, 6-10pm, plus Sun 10am-11.30pm - piano bar.

Botanical, 60 Domain Road, South Yarra, ph 866 1684 - open Mon-Sat noon-1am, Sun noon-11pm - meals daily noon-3pm and from 6pm - trendy pub.

Cherry Tree Hotel, 53 Balmain Street, Richmond, ph 428 5743 - open Tues-Fri 11.30am-1am, Sat 6pm-1am, Sun 11.30am-1am - meals Tues-Fri noon-3pm, Tues-Sat 7-11pm - designer pub.

Gowing's Grace Darling Hotel, cnr Smith & Peel Streets, Collingwood, ph 416 0055 - open Mon-Sat 11am-11pm, Sun noon-8pm - meals seven days noon-2.30pm, and from 6.30pm - a restored colonial bluestone.

Hotham City Diner and Bar, 481 Burwood Road, Hawthorn, ph 819 6090 - open Mon-Sat noon-midnight, Sun 2pm-midnight - meals Mon-Sat noon-2.30pm, nightly 6-10pm - young people's hangout.

McCoppins Hotel, 166 Johnston Street, Fitzroy, ph 417 3427 - open Mon-Tues 11.30am-mid night, Wed-Sat 11.30am-1am, Sun noon-8pm - meals daily noon-2.30pm, Mon-Sat 6.30-9.30pm - deli food with first class wine list.

Smith Street Bar & Bistro, 14 Smith Street, Collingwood, ph 417 2869 - open Mon-Wed noon-midnight, Thurs-Sat noon-2am - bistro Mon-Sat noon-2.30pm, 6.30-10.30pm - bar snacks always available - popular bar.

Comedy

The Comedy Cafe, 175 Brunswick Street, Fitzroy, ph 419 2869 - established in 1979 by a now famous group of comic entertainers - in an 1880s bluestone building - once home of criminal Squizzy Taylor.

Last Laugh Theatre Restaurant/Le Joke, 64 Smith Street, Collingwood, ph 419 8600. Last Laugh open Tues-Sat dinner and show 7.30pm, show only 9pm - one of the original comedy rooms in Melbourne. Le Joke open Tues-Sat dinner and show 7pm, show only 8.30pm.

The Melbourne Comedy Club, 380 Lygon Street, Carlton, ph 348 1622.

Tivoli Theatre Restaurant, 1390 High Street, Malvern, ph 509 9066 - a classy venue with some of the best stand-up comics and situation comedy.

Theatre

Half Tix is in the Bourke Street Mall, ph 650 9420 (recorded message) and is open Mon 10am-2pm, Tues-Thurs 11am-6pm, Fri 11am-6.30pm, Fri 10am-2pm. Discounted tickets are available to many shows, but can only be bought on the day of the performance and paid for in cash.

BASS Entertainment bookings can be arranged by phoning 11 500. Venues include: Anthill Theatre, 199 Napier Street, South Melbourne, ph 699 3253. Athenaeum Theatre, 188 Collins Street, City, ph 650 1500.

Comedy Theatre, 240 Exhibition Street, City, ph 662 2222. Her Majesty's Theatre, 219 Exhibition Street, City, ph 663 3211. La Mama, 205 Faraday Street, Carlton, ph 347 6142. Playbox Theatre Company, 113 Sturt Street, South Melbourne, ph 685 5111. Princess Theatre, 163 Spring Street, City, ph 639 0022. Russell Street Theatre, 19 Russell Street, City, ph 654 4000. Universal Theatre, 19 Victoria Street, Fitzroy, ph 419 3777. Victorian Arts Centre, 100 St Kilda Road, City, ph 617 8211.

Concerts

Fantastic Entertainment in Public Places (FEIPP) presents fabulous, mostly free entertainment throughout Melbourne. Outdoors when it's fine, indoors in winter, ph 663 8395 for what's on when you are there.

Flinders Park National Tennis centre, Flinders Park, Batman Avenue, ph 655 1234.

Victorian Arts Centre, 100 St Kilda Road, ph 617 8211.

Cinemas

• **New releases are screened at:**

Greater Union Russell Cinemas, 131 Russell Street, City, ph 654 8133.

Hoyts Cinema Centre, 140 Bourke Street, City, ph 663 3303.

Hoyts Midcity, 200 Bourke Street, City, ph 663 3081.

Village City Centre, 206 Bourke Street, City, ph 667 6565.

• **Classic films & Art House movies are screened at:**

Astor Theatre, 1 Chapel Street, City, ph 510 1414.

Brighton Bay, 294 Bay Street, North Brighton, ph 596 3590.

Carlton Moviehouse, 235 Faraday Street, Carlton, ph 347 8909.

Kino, Collins Place, 45 Collins Street, City, ph 650 2100.

Longford, 59 Toorak Road, South Yarra, ph 867 2700.

State Film Theatre, 1 Macarthur Street, East Melbourne, ph 651 1490.

Trak, 445 Toorak Road, Toorak, ph 827 9333.

Valhalla, 89 High Street, Northcote, ph 482 2001.

SHOPPING

Melbourne is known as the **shopping capital of Australia**, and you can literally 'shop til you drop'. There are two hundred shops in two city blocks!

Bourke Street is a pedestrian mall (apart from the trams running through its centre) between Swanston and Elizabeth Streets.

Department Stores

David Jones, 310 Bourke Street Mall, City, ph 669 8200, offers quality brands and service second to none.

Georges, 162 Collins Street, City, ph 283 5555, is the last word on Melbourne style.

Myer, 314 Bourke Street Mall, City, ph 66 111, is the fifth largest store in the world with 12 floors of exciting goods.

Daimaru, 211 Latrobe Street, City, ph 660 6666, is Australia's first international department store. It is part of the enormous redevelopment of Melbourne Central.

Arcades

The Block Arcade, 282 Collins Street, City, has traditional tearooms, antique jewellery and designer boutiques.

The Causeway, Bourke Street Mall, City, has jewellery and fashion stores and sidewalk cafes.

Centrepoint Mall, 283 Bourke Street, City, is multi-level mall with fashion and great snack selections.

Royal Arcade, 308 Little Collins Street, City, has giftware, memorabilia and Met information.

The Walk Arcade, Bourke Street Mall, City, has young fashion, homewares and great food.

Shopping Centres

Melbourne's all-under-one-roof shopping complexes are found in the suburbs.

Box Hill Central Shopping Centre, Main Street, Box Hill, ph 890 1000.

Chadstone Shopping Centre, 1341 Dandenong Road, Chadstone, ph 563 3355.

Forest Hill Chase, 270 Canterbury Road, Forest Hill, ph 878 7111.

Highpoint City Shopping Centre, 200 Rosamond Road, Maribyrnong, ph 318 1699.

Jam Factory Shopping Centre, 500 Chapel Street, South Yarra, ph 826 0537.

Knox City Shopping Centre, 425 Burwood Highway, Wantirna South, ph 801 5966.

Malvern Central Shopping Centre, 110 Wattletree Road, Malvern, ph 509 2288.

Northland Shopping Centre, 50 Murray Road, East Preston, ph 478 1399.

Quayside Balmoral Shopping Centre, Rossmith Avenue, Frankston, ph 783 7033.

Westfield Shoppingtowns, 619 Doncaster Road, Doncaster, ph 848 1699; 1239 Nepean Highway, Cheltenham, ph 584 9696; cnr Dromana Avenue & Louis Street, Airport West, ph 338 4244.

Village Shopping

Every village has a theme, which makes comparison shopping easy.

Acland Street, St Kilda, has rows of cake shops and coffee houses, bars and restaurants, all across the road from Luna Park.

Bridge Road & Swan Street, Richmond. The home of factory outlets and seconds stores for the major fashion labels.

Brunswick Street, Fitzroy has everything from 50s revivalist cafes to retro fashion.

Chapel Street, South Yarra-Prahan has many shops offering designer labels and wares from Japan, amongst nightclubs, bars and restaurants. This area is popular for men's fashion goods.

Greville Street, Prahran has a mix of fashion shops from cowboy gear to recycled clothes.

High Street, Armadale, has heaps of antique shops and Persian rug bazaars, along with great restaurants.

Lygon Street, Carlton is in the heart of Little Italy, and has many outlets for Italian fashion and food.

Toorak Road, South Yarra, offers stylish shopping with the world's most sought-after designer labels.

Toorak Road, Toorak is a mecca for the rich and famous, and provides them with life's little luxuries.

Markets

Camberwell Sunday Market, Station Street, Camberwell, ph 509 6706, has second-hand furniture, clothing, china and toys. It is open 8am-1pm.

Esplanade Market, Upper Esplanade, St Kilda, ph 536 1306. An arts and crafts market open Sun 10am-5pm.

Greville Street Sunday Market, Greville Street, Prahran, ph 529 6832. A large rage of goods available noon-5pm.

Prahran Market, 163-185 Commercial Road, South Yarra, ph 522 3302. Fresh produce, meat, poultry and seafood available Tues and Thurs 8am-5pm, Fri 7am-6pm, Sat 7am-1pm.

Queen Victoria Market, cnr Elizabeth & Victoria Streets, Melbourne, ph 658 9600. Over 1000 stalls offer fresh produce, deli goods, clothing and household items. Open Tues and Thurs 6am-2pm, Fri 6am-6pm, Sat 6am-1pm, Sun 9am-4pm (no meat, fish, fruit or vegetables).

South Melbourne Market, cnr York & Coventry Streets, South Melbourne, ph 695 8294, has fresh food, clothing, craft and homewares. Open Wed 7am-2pm, Fri 7am-6pm, Sat 7am-1pm, Sun 8am-4pm.

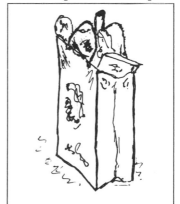

Factory Outlets

It is wise to telephone ahead before visiting any of these outlets, as they do not have regular shopping hours.

Richmond

Absolute Fashion Clearance, 232 Swan Street, Richmond, ph 427 9317.

Abundance, Shop 8, 271 Bridge Road, Richmond, ph 428 8202.

Benetton Factory Outlet, 234 Swan Street, Richmond, ph 428 1160.

Canterbury Clearing Store, 95 Bridge Road, Richmond, ph 427 7343.

Clothesline, 123 Bridge Road, Richmond, ph 428 8794.

Cuggi, 49-53 Coppin Street, Richmond, ph 427 9777.

Dolina Clearance House, 181a Swan Street, Richmond, ph 428 6562.

Fletcher Jones, 165 Swan Street, Richmond, ph 428 0968.

Jill Clegg, 51 Bridge Road, Richmond, ph 428 7902.

Just Jeans, 238 Swan Street, Richmond, ph 427 9265.

Laura Ashley, 236 Swan Street, Richmond, ph 427 9268.

Le Shirt, 185 Bridge Road, Richmond, ph 427 1674.

Mariana Hardwick Clearance, 109 Bridge Road, Richmond, ph 429 4940.

Ojay Clearance, Shop 7, 267-271 Bridge Road, Richmond, ph 427 7834.

Overflow, 193 Swan Street, Richmond, ph 429 5435.

Perfect Imperfects, 205 Bridge Road, Richmond, ph 428 1670.

Sally Browne Samples & Seconds, 227 Bridge Road, Richmond, ph 428 2508.

Sam's Leather, 264 Church Street, Richmond, ph 429 3724.

Stitches, 181 Swan Street, Richmond, ph 429 5791.

Under The Table, 259 Bridge Road, Richmond, ph 428 6329.

Walter Kristensen, 161 Swan Street, Richmond, ph 427 9618.
Weiss Excess, 100 Bridge Road, Richmond, ph 429 8828.

Young Designers Gallery, 28 Bridge Road, Richmond, ph 428 6616.

Other Suburbs

Diana Ferrari Shoes, 81-91 High Street, Preston, ph 480 5399.

Factory Shoe Sales, 180 Grange Road, Fairfield, ph 499 2307.

Givoni, 182 Bay Street, Brighton, ph 596 5828.

Hysport International, 11 Wise Avenue, Seaford, ph 786 8211.

Maternity Warehouse, 487 North Road, Ormond, ph 578 0589.

Michaelis Bayley Footwear, 2 Ryan Street, Footscray, ph 689 4688.

Not 100 Per Cent Shop, 478 Hampton Street, Hampton, ph 597 0237.

Opan Clearance Centre, 283 Chapel Street, Prahran, ph 521 2407.

Rob Paynter, 91 Errol Street, North Melbourne, ph 328 3719.

Sportscraft, 4 Redfern Street, East Hawthorn, ph 811 6666.

Sportscraft Knitwear, 4 Oxley Road, Hawthorn, ph 818 0221.

Taranto Seconds Shop, 288 Johnston Street, Abbotsford, ph 419 2433.

The Stretch Shop, 430 Brunswick Street, Fitzroy, ph 416 1885.

Windsor Smith-Lipstik Shoes, 195 High Street, Preston, ph 480 2455.

Shopping Tours

The following companies offer shopping tours of various areas and duration. Contact the companies direct for full information.

Jackies Shopping Tours, PO Box 299, North Carlton, 3054, ph 347 5655.

Melbourne Shopping Tours, 2 Easey Street, Collingwood, 3066, ph 416 3722.

Shopping Spree Tours, PO Box 40, Huntingdale, 3166, ph 543 5855.

Special Buying Tours, 3/198 Cotham Road, Kew, ph 817 5985.

SIGHTSEEING

City Explorer Bus

Taking a tour on the City Explorer is a good way to get your bearings. It leaves from Flinders Street Station, in Swanston Street, on the hour between 10am and 4pm, and visits most of the main city attractions. You can get off the bus at any stop, then catch a later bus to the next attraction.

Highlights are: St Paul's Cathedral, Cook's Cottage, Fitzroy Gardens, Melbourne Cricket Ground, St Patrick's Cathedral, Old Melbourne Gaol, National Museum, Cosmopolitan Lygon Street, Melbourne University, Royal Melbourne Zoo, Queen Victoria Markets (not Mon or Wed), Shrine of Remembrance, Royal Botanic Gardens, Victorian Arts Centre and National Gallery.

Fares are $13 adult, $6 child, and you can purchase the tickets from the driver. For more information ph 650 1511.

Museum of Victoria

The museum is a fine example of mid-Victorian architecture in the heart of the city. Visitors stroll through spacious galleries to see a series of excellent exhibitions relating to the state's collections. These include exhibitions showing the 40,000 year history of the Aboriginal Koorie culture, the story of Victoria since white settlement, the unique birdlife of Australasia and Antarctica, and Australia's most famous racehorse, Phar Lap. The museum also has a children's section and a Planetarium. Amenities include a coffee shop and a souvenir shop.

Situated at 328 Swanston Street, ph 669 9888, the museum is open daily 10am-5pm (closed Christmas Day, Good Friday and Anzac Day).

Admission is $4 adult, $2 child.

State Library of Victoria

The library opened in 1856, and is on the corner of Swanston and La Trobe Streets, ph 669 9888. It is Victoria's major public reference and research centre, housing a collection of over 12 million items; the largest newspaper collection in Australia; hundreds of thousands of historical paintings and photographs; plus maps, manuscripts and periodicals.

It is open Mon 1-9pm, Tues 10am-6pm, Wed 10am-9pm, Thurs-Sun 10am-6pm (closed public holidays and Dec 25-Jan 1 inclusive).

Old Melbourne Gaol

The gaol was built between 1841-1862 and once covered most of a city block. The National Trust has preserved one remaining cell block as a penal museum, which has a unique collection tracing the story of transportation, convicts, and the development of Victoria's penal system. It is believed that 104 hangings were carried out at the gaol, including that of Ned Kelly, Australia's most infamous bushranger, on November 11, 1880. The museum displays Kelly's unique steel armour, his guns and his death mask. The gaol is in Russell Street, opposite Police Headquarters, ph 663 7228, and is open daily 9.30am-4.30pm (closed Good Friday and Christmas Day).

Admission is $5.50 adult, $2.50 child.

Chinatown

Situated in Little Bourke Street, Chinatown extends from Exhibition Street to Swanston Street. It contains many restaurants from the most economical to the extremely expensive. The Chinese Museum is in 22 Cohen Place, and is one of the best small museums in Melbourne. It is open Sun-Thurs, noon-5pm, ph 662 2888.

Parliament House

The Houses of the Victorian Legislative Council and Legislative Assembly were built in 1856. Situated in Spring Street, at the top of Bourke Street, Melbourne's Parliament House is one of the finest outside of England. Stone from the Grampians (Gariwerd) Mountains in central Victoria was used for the foundations and outer walls. The Council chamber is Neo-Classical in style, with delicate gold leafing on its vaulted ceiling.

Admission is by tour group (eight or more people) only, and guided tours operate Mon-Fri 10am, 11am, noon, 2pm, 3pm and 3.45pm, when Parliament is not in session. For more information, phone 651 8568.

St Patrick's Cathedral

The Gothic Revival Cathedral is in Cathedral Place, which runs off Lansdowne Street, and is constructed from Footscray bluestone. The building was completed in 1897, except for the spires, which were added in 1936. There is a statue in the churchyard of the great Irish liberator, Daniel O'Connell, which is a replica of that which stands in O'Connell Street, Dublin. The Cathedral contains many beautiful works of art.

Fitzroy Gardens

Bounded by Albert, Clarendon, Lansdowne Streets and Wellington Parade in East Melbourne, Fitzroy Gardens are delightful nineteen century gardens, having been laid out in the 1850s.

A main attraction in the

gardens is *Cook's Cottage*, a stone cottage from the village of Great Ayton, Yorkshire, England, which was the home of Captain Cook's parents. The cottage was dismantled in 1933 and transported to Australia for reconstruction to mark Melbourne's centenary in 1934. The ivy presently covering the cottage walls was grown from an original snip taken from Great Ayton.

The cottage is open daily 9am-5pm (5.30pm during Daylight Saving) except Christmas day, ph 419 8742. **Admission is $2 adult, $1 child.**

Also in the gardens are the famous Fairy Tree and the miniature Tudor Village replica. Adjacent to Fitzroy Gardens are the Treasury Gardens containing the John F. Kennedy Memorial.

Australian Gallery of Sport & Olympic Museum/MCG

The gallery is at the members' entrance to the Melbourne Cricket Ground in Jolimont Terrace, Jolimont, ph 654 8922.

The Gallery and MCG reflect Melbourne's claim as Australia's sporting capital. Both areas hold a fascinating collection of items and memorabilia from sports including cricket, Australian football, cycling, tennis, boxing, lawn bowls, rowing, hockey, lacrosse and yachting.

The Olympic Museum contains a permanent exhibition from the first modern Olympics in Athens in 1896 to the 1992 Games in Barcelona.

The complex has a theatrette showing continuous sporting videos. There is also a coffee shop and souvenir shop.

Tours of the MCG are included on non-match days. The gallery is open Tues-Sat 10am-4pm, and admission is $3 adult, $1 child.

Through the Melbourne Sports Network, a telephone call to the Gallery of Sport provides access to tours of major sporting venues, utilization of playing surfaces, and tickets for major sporting events.

National Tennis Centre

At the National Tennis Centre Flinders Park, ph 655 1234, you can play tennis, visit the pro-shop or coffee lounge, have professional coaching, or simply take a tour Mon-Thurs at 11am, noon or 1.30pm. **The tours cost $3, and playing prices are available on application.**

Olympic Park

Tours of the Olympic Park Complex, including the Melbourne Sports and Entertainment Centre, offer: hire of sports grounds, equipment, change room and gym facilities; coaching sessions for soccer, hockey, athletics and lacrosse; **individual use of athletics track/gym/sauna/change room for $1.**
 There is a charge of $1 for a tour of facilities. The No. 2 Ground may be hired for $35 per hour for training.

State Swimming Centre

The centre is the home of Victorian water sports and it offers: use of the 50m pool; the diving pool; gymnasium facilities; coaching in swimming, diving and water polo (for interested groups). **Tours are available for $1, and there is a gym/sauna /swim package for $5.10.**

Queen Victoria Gardens and Kings Domain

These were originally the site of a gold-rush shanty town, which was proclaimed public parkland in 1854. The area contains Australian and English trees, and one of the most attractive sections of the Kings Domain is a garden of rockeries, tiny paths and waterfalls which commemorate the Pioneer Women of Victoria.
 The well-known *Floral Clock*, whose floral design is changed four times a year requiring the planting of over 30,000 flowers, is in the Queen Victoria Gardens.

The Sydney Myer Music Bowl

Venue for many of Melbourne's popular entertainment events, the Bowl is in the Kings Domain, and can accommodate over 50,000 people within the shell and on the surrounding lawns. Admission to a concert at the Bowl is $6.80 adults.

Shrine of Remembrance

Dedicated to the sacrifice made by Victorian men and women in the two world wars, the Shrine is also in the Kings Domain. It was built to honour the dead of the First World War, with the foundation stone being laid in 1927, and the dedication taking place in 1934. The building was designed by Architects P.B. Hudson and J.H. Wardrop.

A feature is the Stone of Remembrance, the centre of which is illuminated by a shaft of sunlight at exactly

11am on Armistice Day, November 11 each year.

The inner Shrine is open Mon-Sat 10am-5pm.

La Trobe's Cottage

The cottage is in the Domain, on the corner of Birdwood Avenue and Dallas Brooks Drive, South Yarra, and was the colony's first Government House. La Trobe brought the house out with him in the ship *Fergusson*, along with his family and other possessions.

Charles Joseph La Trobe was Lieutenant-Governor of Victoria between 1851-1854, and the National Trust supervised the re-creation of the house, which contains many of the original furnishings.

The cottage is open Sat-Thurs 11am-4.30pm (11am-2.30pm July and August), ph 654 5528. **Admission is $5 adult, $2.50 child.**

Victoria's present Government House has been the State's vice-regal residence since 1876. It features a state ballroom, musicians' gallery, the largest collection of late Victorian antiques in Australia, and magnificent gardens.

Tours of the current Government House can be arranged (subject to availability) on Mon, Wed and Sat, ph 654 4562.

Royal Botanic Gardens Melbourne

This beautiful garden was established in 1846, and displays a diverse collection of over 10,000 plant species and cultivars in a glorious 19th century landscape. The collection is organised into thematic, geographical and horticultural displays.

The Australian Collection is a must for overseas visitors. Information and orientation are available at the Visitor Centre within the Herbarium Building on Birdwood Ave. Souvenirs can be purchased at the Friends' shop, and the Tea Rooms overlooking the Lake offer lunches, Devonshire teas and snacks. Free guided walks leave the Visitor centre at 10am and 11am on Tues-Fri and Sun.

The gardens are situated between Alexandra and Birdwood Avenues, South Yarra, ph 655 2341.

Victorian Arts Centre Complex

A short walk from Melbourne's central business district, and across St Kilda Road from the Queen Victoria Gardens, the Victorian Arts Centre sits on the south bank of the Yarra River. The Centre comprises the State Theatre, Playhouse, George Fairfax Studio, Melbourne Concert Hall, Westpac Gallery and Performing Arts Museum. In addition, original artworks are a feature of the foyers.

The centre is open daily (except Good Friday and Christmas Day) and guided tours operate Sun-Fri, with **Backstage tours available on Sun - $10 (not available for children under 12).**

The South Bank of the Yarra has recently been extensively redeveloped with a wide assortment of grand buildings, shopping and a riverside walk. There are many outdoor cafes where you can take a well-earned break from sightseeing.

National Gallery of Victoria

The gallery, at 180 St Kilda Road, adjacent to the Victorian Arts Centre, has one of the finest collections of art in the southern hemisphere.

There are over 70,000 works, including Aboriginal, Asian, Australian, European, pre-Columbian and Contemporary art, including paintings, sculptures, photographs, decorative arts, prints and drawings.

The world renowned Great Hall of the gallery has the largest stained glass ceiling in the world.

The gallery is open daily 10am-5pm (closed Christmas Day, Good Friday and Anzac Day morning). Admission is $4.50 adult, $2 child.

Princes Bridge

Princes Bridge is Melbourne's oldest and grandest, and crosses the Yarra where Swanston Street becomes St Kilda Road. It was built around 1886, replacing a wooden bridge that had been opened by La Trobe in 1850.

Flinders Street Station

Although this station, on the corner of Flinders and Swanston Streets, has been the centre of the city's train system since 1854, the building was only completed in 1909-10. The station has been extensively remodelled and electronic timetables have been installed. So, you might wonder, why the clocks

at the entrance? Well, it seems that in days gone by it was the done thing to arrange to meet people 'under the clocks', so when plans were afoot to remove them there was a public outcry from people who had fond memories of their special meeting place.

The station is not really very important to Melburnians now, but **visitors usually like to have their photograph taken on the front steps.**

Young & Jackson's Hotel

Also known as Princes Bridge Hotel, the pub is at 1 Swanston Street. Its claim to fame is that the upstairs lounge is home to the infamous painting 'Chloe' which caused such a public outcry when it was first hung in the Melbourne Art Gallery in the 1880s.

She may have caused a stir then, but now she hardly manages to raise an eyebrow.

St Paul's Cathedral

The Gothic Revival Anglican Cathedral is on the corner of Swanston and Flinders Street, on the site of the first official church service in Melbourne. The Cathedral was completed in 1891, and the spires added between 1926 and 1931.

Capitol Theatre

The ceiling of the theatre, at 113 Swanston Street, was designed by Walter Burley Griffin, the architect of the city of Canberra.

Melbourne Town Hall

The Town Hall, on the corner of Swanston and Collins Streets, was built between 1867 and 1870, and the portico was added in 1887. It is worth going inside the main hall to see the chandeliers, murals and organ. The Town Hall was one of the main venues for concerts before the advent of the Concert Hall in St Kilda Road.

Polly Woodside Maritime Park

The park is in Phayer Street, South Melbourne, ph 699 9760.

The barque *Polly Woodside* is a deep-water, square-rigged, commercial sailing ship built of riveted iron in 1885. Built in Belfast, she is now moored in the original Duke's and Orr's Dry Dock, outside a nautical museum which portrays Melbourne's maritime heritage and the development of shipping. In 1988, the barque was the sixth ship in the world to be awarded a World Ship Trust Heritage Medal for excellence in restoration.

The museum is open Mon-Fri 10am-4pm, Sat-Sun 10am- 5pm (closed Good Friday and Christmas Day) and admission is $7 adult, $4 child.

A licensed restaurant serves lunches and Devonshire teas.

Yarra Cruises

Leisurely cruises on a river boat can be arranged through Melbourne River Tours, ph Mon-Fri 629 7233, Sat Sun 650 2055. They leave from Princes Walk, cnr Princes Bridge and Batman Avenue. Examples of the many tours available are:

1. Port of Melbourne - 1 1/4 hours - $11 adult, $5.50 child.

See Melbourne's proud maritime past and modern docklands. Experience the early settlement days with views of quaint old docks, the barque *Polly Woodside*, and bluestone wharves that evoke images of the boom years of the gold rush, framed by the towering city skyline.

2. Herring Island - 1 1/4 hours - **$11 adult, $5.50 child.**

Glide past the grand old trees of Alexandra Avenue and the world famous Botanical Gardens, the Olympic Stadium, Melbourne Cricket Ground and Tennis Centre.

3. A combination of 1. and 2. - 2 3/4 hours - **$21 adult, $10 child.**

Royal Melbourne Zoological Gardens

The zoo is about 4km from the city in Elliott Avenue, Parkville, ph 285 9300. It is open daily 9am-5pm, with later closing some evenings during summer. **Admission is $9 adult, $4.50 child.** Tram 55 will take you from William and Peel Streets in the city to the zoo gates. Other trams will take you to the general area, but this one travels through Royal Park, which is not open to cars, and is a very scenic journey.

The animals are displayed in naturalistic landscaped settings, and highlights include the Butterfly House, the Gorilla Rainforest, the Great Flight Aviary, and the Treetop Monkey Exhibit. Melbourne Zoo breeds and exhibits many rare and endangered species, including Lowland Gorillas, Snow Leopards, Sumatran Tigers, Tree Kangaroos and Crocodiles.

For sustenance there are snack shops and a restaurant, and there is also a souvenir shop.

University of Melbourne

Also in Parkville, although some might argue that its address should be Carlton, is the University of Melbourne. Building was begun in the early 1850s, and it hit the headlines when the workers downed tools and took part in a march to the city demonstrating for an eight-hour working day.

The university has some interesting museums and galleries: Percy Grainger Museum, near Gate 8 on Royal Parade, open Mon-Fri 10am-4pm; University Gallery, near Union House, open Mon-Fri 10am-5pm, until 7pm on Wed; the George Paton Gallery in Union House, open Mon-Tues & Thurs 10am-6pm, Wed noon-7.30pm, Fri 1-6pm. Union House also has a snack bar.

Exhibition Building

A complex of buildings covering 8ha was built for the International Exhibition of 1880, but only the main hall now remains, in the picturesque Carlton Gardens. The huge dome roof was modelled on the cathedral in Florence, and a matching roof was to have been erected on nearby Sacred Heart Church in Rathdowne Street, but it never eventuated.

The Exhibition Building was the site of the opening of the first Federal Parliament in

1901. It is now only open when exhibitions are being held, but you can explore the outside.

St Kilda

St Kilda was Melbourne's equivalent to Sydney's Kings Cross, but it has cleaned up its act and is now home to a bohemian/arty set.

From Swanston Street, there are many trams that run to St Kilda, and from Collins Street, Trams 10 and 12 go through South Melbourne to St Kilda. By road, St Kilda is reached by the West Gate Freeway from the west, Punt Road from the north.

The Esplanade runs along the beach, which is not renowned for its waves, and leads to the St Kilda Pier, which has a kiosk built in 1904. The St Kilda hot sea baths are nearby, and are very popular.

Along with the shops and restaurants, the main attraction is probably **Luna Park** in Cavell Street, which is a fun park that has been operating since the 1920s. **It is now open Sat 1.30-5.15pm, Sun noon-5.45pm, Fri-Sat 7.30-11.15pm, and during school holidays also Mon-Fri 1.30-5.15pm.** There is no admission charge, but if you want to go on any rides **the charges are $14 adults, $11 children under 14, for unlimited rides.**

Opposite Luna Park, on the corner of Cavell Street and Lower Esplanade, is the *Palais Theatre*, which was originally built in 1915, but burnt down during the 1920s. Mr H.E. White, an American, designed the new Palais, with seating for nearly 3000 people.

TOURS

The three big coach tour companies are:

AAT King's, 108 Ireland Street, West Melbourne, ph 329 8022.

Australian Pacific Tours, 181 Flinders Street, ph 650 1511.

Pioneer Gray Line, 181 Flinders Street, ph 654 7700.

They basically offer the same tours, with a only few variations, and pick-up from your hotel, or somewhere very close to it, can be arranged.

Following is a selection of day tours available, with prices that should be used as a guide only.

Melbourne Sights, Parks & Gardens - departs daily 2pm, returning approx 5.30pm.
Adults $33, children $31.
Comprehensive city tour.

City, Dandenongs, Sherbrooke Forest - departs daily 9am, returning approx 12.30pm.
Adults $33, children $31.
See the city highlights, and travel through the eastern suburbs to the Dandenong Ranges, Sylvan Dam and the Sherbrooke Forest.

City Sights and Penguins - departs daily 2pm, returning approx 11.30pm.
Adults $76, children $67.50.
Visits all the important sights in the city then travels to Phillip Island to watch the evening fairy penguin parade.

City Sights, Dandenongs and Penguins - departs daily 9am, returning approx 11.30pm.
Adults $85.50, children $75.
Take in the city sights, the Dandenong Ranges, the bayside suburbs of Brighton and Beaumaris, then travel across the Mornington Peninsula to Phillip Island. Dinner is available at Cowes before returning to Melbourne via Cranbourne.

Ballarat Wildlife Park, Sovereign Hill - departs daily 9am, returning approx 5.30pm.
Adults $67.50, children $62.50.
Travel through Bacchus Marsh to the Wildlife and Reptile Park for a conducted tour, then continue on to Sovereign Hill, a restored gold-mining township. Lunch is available at the United States Hotel or the New York Bakery, then after

touring Sovereign Hill, visit Ballarat, see the site of the Eureka Stockade, visit the botanical gardens and Lake Wendouree, before returning to Melbourne.

Sovereign Hill Sound & Light Show - departs Wed & Sat (Jan-May) 5.30pm, returning approx 11.30pm.
Adults $77 (with dinner) $55 (without dinner), children $74 and $52.
The smorgasbord meal is served at Charlie Napier Hotel. Those not wishing to avail themselves of this opportunity are transferred to Ballarat where there are several eateries.

"Puffing Billy", Wildlife and Wine-Tasting - departs daily 9am, returning approx 5.30pm.
Adults $78.50, children $74 (includes spit roast lunch).
Travel through the eastern suburbs to Ferntree Gully and the Blue Dandenongs. At Belgrave, board "Puffing Billy", the oldest steam railway still operating in Australia, and travel to Menzies Creek. Continue on through the Yarra Valley for wine-tasting and lunch at Fergusson's Winery. In the afternoon visit Healesville Wildlife Sanctuary.

Great Ocean Road, Port Campbell National Park - departs Tues-Wed, Fri-Sun 9am, returning approx 9.30pm.
Adults $71.50, children $65.
Travel across the Westgate Bridge to Geelong, then on to Torquay and the start of the Great Ocean Road, one of the world's great coastal roads. Travel through Anglesea and Lorne, then stop for lunch at Apollo Bay. Cross the Otway Ranges and enter Port Campbell National Park, home of the Twelve Apostles, the remains of London Bridge and the Loch Ard Gorge.
This trip can be extended to two days, with overnight accommodation at Lorne - adults $225, children $203.

Grampians National Park, Kangaroos, Koalas - departs Thurs & Sun 9am, returning approx 9.45pm.
Adults $67, children $61.
Drive through Bacchus Marsh, Ballarat and Ararat to the Grampians National Park. Visit the Mackenzie Falls and Lake Bellfield, Hall's Gap and the Brambuk Aboriginal Cultural Centre, where you can sample bush tucker. Return to Melbourne via Stawell, site of the well-known Stawell Easter Gift foot-race, and Great Western, the champagne town.

SPORT

Football

Melbourne is the head-quarters of *Australian Football*, which was previously known as Australian (or Aussie) Rules. In States where this particular code of football is not as popular, it is also known as "Aerial Ping-Pong", but it is not suggested that you use that name when in Melbourne. It is a very fast game, similar to *Gaelic Football*, and in fact, on occasions Gaelic teams visit Melbourne and games are played following one set of rules for the first half, and the other rules for the second half. If you are in Melbourne on a Saturday in winter, it is worth attending a match even if you don't understand what is going on. The atmosphere is electric, and people turn up in their hundreds of thousands to cheer for their teams. **Details of matches and venues can be found in the sporting pages of the newspapers, or just ask someone on the street for the closest ground to where you are staying.** The main venues are the MCG and VFL Park at Waverley Park.

Soccer is also played in Melbourne, but it doesn't have as large a following as Australian Football. The main venue is Olympic Park, Swan Street, City. *Rugby* also has a small faithful band of supporters.

Horse Racing

Melbourne has four venues for horse racing:
Flemington in Epsom Road, Flemington;
Caulfield in Station Street, Caulfield;
Moonee Valley in McPherson Street, Moonee Ponds; and
Sandown in Racecourse Dr., Springvale.
   Harness Racing's main venue is Moonee Valley, and races are held every Saturday night and some Mondays.

Cricket

During summer many International Tests, one day Internationals, and Sheffield Shield Cricket matches are played at the Melbourne Cricket Ground (MCG), Yarra Park, Jolimont. First grade cricket is played at many suburban grounds, and details are in the daily newspapers.

Greyhound Racing

There are two venues for this sport - Olympic Park on Monday nights, and Sandown Park on Thursday nights.

Tennis

The Australian Tennis Open is held each year at the National Tennis Centre in Batman Avenue, East Melbourne, ph 655 1234.

If you wish to hire a court to have a hit yourself, the Yellow Pages of the Telephone Directory has a list under "Tennis Courts for Hire".

Golf

The Johnnie Walker Classic is held at Royal Melbourne, Cheltenham Road, Black Rock, ph 598 6755, but the course is not available for visitors. You can get a game across the road, though, at Sandringham Municipal Golf Links, Cheltenham Road, Cheltenham, ph 598 3590.

There are many picturesque golf courses in Melbourne, particularly the Huntingdale Golf Club, Windsor Avenue, Oakleigh East, ph 579 4622, and **information on available venues** can be found in the Yellow Pages of the Telephone Director under "Clubs - Golf", or "Golf Courses - Public".

Speedway

Calder Park Thunderdome, Calder Highway, Keilor, is Australia's only super speedway. Info, ph 390 1222.

Motor Cycle

Races are held at the Phillip Island Motor Racing Circuit, ph (059) 522 710 for details of forthcoming meetings.

The Yellow Pages of the Telephone Directory has information on facilities for all other sports.

INDEX